Insight for Adult Learning Groups

Module 24

General Editor: David G. Hamilton

Why does God allow suffering?

Andrew Knock

Insight for Adult Learning Groups

Module 24

General Editor: David G. Hamilton

Marshall Pickering

An Imprint of HarperCollins*Publishers*

Marshall Pickering is an Imprint of
HarperCollins *Religious*
Part of HarperCollins *Publishers*
77–85 Fulham Palace Road, London W6 8JB

First published in Great Britain
in 1996 by Marshall Pickering

1 3 5 7 9 10 8 6 4 2

A catalogue record for this book is
available from the British Library

0 551 030402

Printed and bound in Great Britain by
Woolnough Bookbinding Ltd, Irthlingborough, Northamptonshire

Contents

Preface vi

Introduction vii

Session 1   The Bible and human experience 1

Session 2   Protection or a new creation? 7

Session 3   Suffering and reconciliation 12

Session 4   Self-giving and prayer 17

Preface

INSIGHT is a learning programme for the *whole* Church. It incorporates learning resources for use with children, teenagers, younger adults, adult learning groups, intergenerational groups and church holiday clubs for young people. Its locus is the community of faith, people of all ages engaged in worshipping, learning and serving God together. The programme offers a wide range of learning modules for each of the constituent groups and encourages congregational leaders to identify the needs of their people and to construct their own parish education programme on a *pick 'n' mix* basis using the modules. The scheme is outlined in the *INSIGHT Handbook* and *INSIGHT for Church Leaders*.

The modules in this series of volumes, *INSIGHT for Adult Learning Groups*, offer a wide range of studies which range in content from the personal and pastoral needs of individuals to the major social issues of the day and the challenge to Christians to engage in creative and redemptive discipleship. Some adult learning groups may be attracted also to the options available in the series of titles in the companion series, *INSIGHT for Younger Adults*.

The series has been developed by Parish Education Publications in partnership with HarperCollins*Religious*.

DAVID G. HAMILTON
GENERAL EDITOR

Introduction

The question *Why does God allow suffering?* is almost always near the heart of the complaint put out by non-Christians, to express their unwillingness to join a church. It is probably not the actual reason why they do not join – more often than not, the reason is the church itself. But many people want to know more of God; for them the question is very real.

This course is an attempt to lead ordinary members of congregations to be better equipped to respond to the question. It is not written, however, as an exercise in apologetics, but more in the desire to ask 'What is God *like*?'. In some cases it may enable people to be the 'face of Christ' to non-Christians, signs for them of a different kind of God.

The course is intended for use by non-specialist groups, both congregational and ecumenical. It does not summarise every answer to the questions which Christian tradition has provided, but explores various twentieth-century approaches in an original and illuminating way.

It is set out in four sessions, and may be completed in four evening meetings of 2–2½ hours. Equally, the material may be reorganised for a longer course. For example, some groups may wish to set aside an additional one or two meetings, in case the group wishes to explore a particular issue in more depth. As with all *INSIGHT* programmes, flexibility is the key.

All participants should try to read through a session before the meeting. Some groups may wish to read through the text aloud before working on each question. Others may ask various participants to summarise each section of text leading up to a question, and then set aside time to discuss that text as well.

Each group member should be equipped with a pen and paper or notebook for completing the exercises in each of the sessions.

The Bible and human experience

To identify some of our most common assumptions about God, the Bible, and suffering, and to ask how we try to support these assumptions.

Why is this happening to me?

One of the most basic of human assumptions is that in a truly *good* life, suffering would not occur. Therefore, if it *does* occur, somehow it must be deserved as a consequence of wrongdoing. Hindu and Buddhist doctrines of *karma* and reincarnation teach that anyone's present life is a direct result of good and bad actions in a previous life. A similar attitude has also prevailed throughout Israel's history. Ezekiel had to argue forcefully against the assumption that a father's sins produce suffering in his sons' lives (Ezekiel 18); and Jesus contradicted the assumption that when Galileans were tortured by Pilate or 18 innocent people at Siloam were crushed by a tower, this was because they must have committed some dreadful sin (Luke 13:1–5).

Often, in extreme situations, people turn to God as a personal insurance against suffering: 'God protects *me*' – regardless of what may happen to other people. For example, in the aftermath of an horrific plane crash in the USA in 1993, in which all passengers and crew were killed, a young man gave an emotional TV interview in which he related how he and his wife were booked on the flight – and were even in the terminal on time – yet somehow, through providence, did not board the plane. 'There is a God, there is a God!' the man repeated exultantly, thinking of the fortune in his own life whilst overlooking the dreadful events of the evening and their consequences to the lives of the victims'

families and friends. Christians are just as prone to this 'me-centred' attitude to God's will and providence as anyone else, and one of the aims of this course is to lead us beyond it.

Suffering and its causes

The word 'suffering' has a number of different meanings, but one aspect they have in common is that, in suffering, people are passive. Suffering happens *to* people, whether as a consequence of other people's actions (be they deliberate or unintentional: wars, criminal violence or the bad stewardship and exploitation of the planet's resources), natural disasters (weather phenomena, earthquakes, volcanoes, diseases) or the 'wages of sin' (wrong living, which leads to ill health, spirals of despair and depression, anxiety, material poverty and humiliation).

These passive forms of suffering are not deliberately chosen, even though some are actually caused by human beings. There is, however, a further kind of suffering – one which is *chosen* – which we will consider in more detail later. Jesus lived a life of *active* suffering, redeeming others. He lived out fully that life which Isaiah had prophesied to be one of God's 'suffering servant', transforming people and events by *suffering them*.

The Bible and suffering

There are some radically different ideas about God and suffering at different points in the Bible which seem to contradict one another:

1) Satan/evil causes human suffering, at least some of the time (God said to Satan, 'Job is in your hands', Job 1:12; 2:6).
2) God causes every disaster ('I, the Lord, bring prosperity and create disaster', Amos 3:6; Isaiah 45:7).
3) God does not want suffering (Isaiah 65:20–3). But he endures the suffering and evil of the world, until he brings about a final end, the 'Day of the Lord' (Jesus's parable of the wheat and weeds, Matthew 13:24–30, 36–43). Facing up to suffering can be a kind of test or purification of God's people, although God does not cause the testing (James 1:3, 12).

4) God is, in Christ, actively overcoming the evils of the world today, including natural disasters (Romans 8:21), and has enlisted Christ's disciples in the battle. Victory is assured, but lies in the future (John 16:33; 1 Corinthians 15:54–57). In parts of the New Testament (notably 1 John and Revelation) 'victory' is not total cosmic victory but an individual's personal victory of righteousness, a sign of victory which the children of God reveal in today's troubled world (1 John 5:4–7).

How do we handle such diversity – even contradiction – in the Bible? We shall explore this question in some depth in this session. However, it is important for us to see at the outset of the course that the basis and *primary* source for our understanding of who God is, and how he acts, is Jesus himself. The revelations of God in the rest of the Bible certainly show us something of God's will and character, and also how God's people have responded to him. For any Christian, however, Jesus's words 'Anyone who has seen me has seen the Father' (John 14:9) are the new starting point for understanding other passages.

Question 1 (10 minutes)

In threes

Discuss your present views about the suffering in the world. Ask in particular:

- Does God cause suffering to occur?
- Does he cause people – for example, babies – to die?
- Does good come out of suffering?
- If so, does the good outcome justify the suffering, or is it really a tribute to the way God's Spirit and human spirits react to adversity?

Ask if a member of the group can relate an example from his or her life when some suffering occurred which he or she believed to have been caused by God. What have the consequences been since then?

Together

Share any points you wish with the whole group.

How is God 'almighty'?

The word 'almighty' is used as a title for God in Scripture. It translates the Hebrew word *shaddai*, used 48 times in the Old Testament (30 of these in the book of *Job*). Because it is a title – a name as much as an adjective – it can be understood in various ways; most translators agree that it has the meaning of the power to injure and protect, particularly with a promise of blessing on the descendants of Abraham.

Question 2 (15 minutes)

Together

If participants are unfamiliar with the book of Job, try to read the beginning and end, if not more, before the meeting. Ask some of the participants to summarise their impressions of the book.

In threes

- Job is described again and again as a man of very great faith. Does this protect him from suffering?
- Does God allow Job to suffer in order to test him, or to prove Satan wrong?
- Have a look at the climax of the book (chapters 38–41, and especially 42:1–6). Does God's 'almightiness' mean that he rescues his faithful servants from suffering, or that he is 'too wonderful' (42:3) for such earthbound concerns?

Together

Share any points you wish with the whole group.

The Bible and the power of God

The Jewish title 'almighty' – *shaddai* – seemed to imply a promise of blessing and protection on the chosen people. Yet it changed its character as Israel lost status and prestige, was exiled and even lost its promised land. There was a promise of restoration; but Jesus transformed it from a promise to only a remnant of Jews to a promise for *anyone* who believed in him – Jew or Gentile – and not only those who were blood descendants of Abraham. Much of Paul's ministry involved explaining this radical change in the 'Old Covenant' to his fellow Jews and to Gentiles.

Just as in Jesus's own case, protection from suffering is not what God provides – as Peter had to learn when he tried to protect Jesus from attack, and as the Church learned in persecution (Mark 8:31–33; John 18:10–11, etc.). We should note in passing that protection from *evil* – for example, the 'armour of God' depicted in Ephesians 6:10–18 – is a proper but different kind of protection. To explore this is beyond the scope of this study.

The Bible shows us a continuing revelation of God's will and nature. Different passages and books relate to different situations. Old Testament ideas of God and how God works have to be reinterpreted in the light of his full revelation in Jesus Christ.

Question 3 (15 minutes)

In (different) threes

Most of us hold a number of assumptions about the Bible and its authority, based on everything from our recollection of Sunday School lessons to a recent personal experience which brought us to listen to Scripture in a new way. Explore some of the following questions about the Bible, selecting the most appropriate for your group.

- If the Bible is inspired by God, does every sentence have equal weight and authority, or do some parts have more authority than others? If so, which parts? Do the parts which explicitly reveal Jesus have the most authority?
- Does each part of the Bible have a different purpose, for example, where God speaks to different people in their own situations?
- Do Christians sometimes turn the Bible, which is the essential doorway into God's life, into 'God' himself, revering the book rather than the person?

Together

Briefly share any personal discoveries made in each group.

Voices of protest

Many people today, including millions of Christians living under the injustice of cruel governments and poverty, would echo the famous words of the character Ivan Karamazov in Dostoyevsky's *The Brothers Karamazov*: 'I don't want any more suffering.'

As Christians, we are unconvincing witnesses to God's power if we seem to be claiming that he uses a 'behind-the-scenes' kind of power, pulling all the strings, particularly when we are faced with someone who cries out in pain and loss, 'How can an almighty God allow my child to die/my country to be butchered/my husband to develop dementia …?'. These cries show us what the word 'almighty' usually means for those people who are not aware of the narrow biblical meaning of the word. For them, and doubtless for many Christians today, it tends to mean *the power to protect us from pain and loss.* And the evidence before their eyes is unmistakable: either he cannot be 'almighty', or if he *is*, he is so cold and hard-hearted that they reject him.

Perhaps it would be better to say that they reject a particular *picture* of him, often picked up in childhood conversations. As the cricketer Dennis Compton wisely observed, usually when someone thinks that he or she no longer believes in God, it is a particular picture of God that is being rejected. Part of the work of Christian ministry should therefore be to help such people move on to a better picture, a more reliable starting point for their exploration of God.

Question 4 (5–8 minutes)

In twos

Discuss whether you have, or have had, some 'pictures' of God or assumptions about him which you want to protest against. Have you checked the pictures against God as revealed in Jesus? Can you recollect times when you moved on from one picture of him to another?

Together

Share some examples, as you wish.

Protection or a new creation?

To begin to explore the distinctive Christian understanding of the power of suffering, and to ask whether God is in control of the world.

The way of love

Many Christian groups and sects today, as for most of the Church's history, answer the cry with which we ended Session 1 – 'Why does God allow such suffering if he is almighty?' – by saying, 'God has grown tired of this sinful world, and will shortly end it.'

At the same time, among many other Christians, there is also a growing awareness that the God fully revealed in Jesus Christ is not like this. In other words, some of the popular images of what God is like, as found even in popular belief, are not true to the revelation of God in Jesus Christ. God may be a disturber, but he is not a destroyer of what he creates or sustains. He may insist on the 'labour pains', as Paul calls them, of repentance and new birth, but he wants his children to be born again, not to die. He is not a tyrant or a killer who 'takes little children'. As we have already noted, when considering the different biblical ideas about God and suffering, our basic standard should be, 'Does *Jesus* reveal God in this way or that?'

Many missionaries, teachers and thinkers in the churches have come to see that God gives his world and its people much greater freedom than is usually portrayed by the Church. God is not a bully. He does not force his will, or his changes, on the world or its people. Rather, he aims constantly to woo the world into joining with him in living out his purposes and will.

God's way is the way of love, not of force. Love embraces, struggles, suffers and empowers; it does not turn away, dominate, reduce or overpower. Many of us may sometimes long for a power of some kind to come and solve our worldly problems today. We have a strong desire for protection; for example, industrial and armed protection as demonstrated by many political developments in underdeveloped industrial nations. However human it may seem, we must take stock of the fact that the self-revelation of God in Jesus is *not* a revelation of this kind of power or this kind of solution. If we are attracted by it, we are attracted by something other than God: an idol.

The power of active suffering

For the New Testament writers, to suffer meant to 'receive', 'embrace' or 'endure', and has a largely positive and active meaning rather than the passive sense we give it today. The King James translation, 'Suffer the little children to come unto me' (Luke 18:16), conveys this sense well; it is an active 'making yourself available' sense – a self-giving. God has an infinite capacity for suffering; indeed, he could not truly love without it. Luke displays this characteristic of God very powerfully: God waits, as the father of the Prodigal Son waited (Luke 15:11–32), enduring the degradation and disappointment of his children, until they turn back. But the father had not been passive, he had already given the younger son his inheritance. His waiting is based on his earlier generosity.

With infinite patience, God woos his errant children back to a new beginning in their lives. He knows that real change cannot be imposed from the outside; it can only come about from within. Persuading them by force would only paper over the cracks. The persuasion is the work of the Spirit of God. In the parable of the Prodigal Son, this is the work of the 'inheritance' which his father so selflessly gives him – to work from within, like a 'fifth column'.

The New Testament introduces us to a new and very positive understanding of suffering. It is active, rather than passive. It means receiving the hurts and blows that others deal out when you reveal the life of God to them (rather than reacting against them), so that a reconciliation is forged.

Question 1 (10 minutes)

On your own

> Have you ever been able to receive another's hurts and not retaliate, yet seek to deepen your relationship with the same person? Were you seeking to share something of God's life with them, and do you think this made your reconciliation more natural? Note the example.

Together

> Briefly share any points you wish to raise.

A Jewish response

> Unlike most Christians, the Jewish people have already experienced a massive and destructive general catastrophe – the Holocaust, the Nazis' concerted attempt at genocide. For many Jews after the Second World War, moreover, Auschwitz and Belsen became symbolic proof that God is not in charge; that Bible passages like Psalm 91, though they show something of God's way, cannot be used as a guarantee of security at all.
>
> For some Jews, the response was to stop expecting God to provide for them at all, and to take charge of their own destiny in the militant Zionism which led to the creation of the political state of Israel. More recently, some senior rabbis have developed a form of teaching about the immortality of the soul, surviving beyond earthly events.
>
> What is striking about these recent responses to God's manifest *lack* of protection for the Jews is that neither response actually says anything *about God,* or what *he* is doing in and for his world. They are typical expressions of the wider world's responses to the major issues which face it: either to seek human solutions to human problems, or to encourage people to escape into individualistic, self-serving religions or pseudo-religious mystical psychologies.
>
> These two responses are widespread in secular society today. We either concentrate on human expertise, without considering God's activity at all, or restrict our religious interest to individualistic, 'me-centred' needs and preferences.

Question 2 (10 minutes)

In threes

- Can you identify with one or both of these responses at least some of the time? Share your reactions.
- What do you believe about death and immortality? Are you more concerned with what happens to you, or with the life of God?

Together

Briefly share any pertinent points with the whole group.

Does God cause *everything* to happen?

So far, we have been asking questions about God's involvement in human suffering. This helps us to recognise that the ways in which people respond to these questions are usually based on their assumptions about even bigger issues.

Very often, people believe that God causes suffering because he causes *everything* to happen anyway. Christians who want to support this view often quote from Ephesians 1:11 saying, 'All things are done according to God's plan and decision.' The passage is used to justify a kind of fatalism about life. Everything that happens must have been planned and caused by God. People have to learn to submit to what happens.

Many of us have a strong human desire – a need, even – to believe that God is in control of all these events. However, when a Christian asserts this view, it is particularly confusing as a witness to non-Christians: they can see that it does not seem to be true in practice, and also seems to ignore God's priceless gift of human freedom. Even more seriously, Jesus did not show us that our world is completely under God's control. Instead, he taught us to pray for the *Kingdom to come*, the word 'Kingdom' meaning God's reign, rule or authority. It is coming, it is breaking in, but it is *not* here yet! Many other forces and powers also affect the world at the moment. We may rightly be confident that God's rule will operate everywhere, but this should never lead us into deliberate blindness to the present mixture of order and chaos.

The quotation from Ephesians 1:11 is poorly translated in the *Good News Bible*. Its meaning becomes clearer when we read it together with verse 9: 'God *did* [or revealed] *what he purposed* [or planned].' In other words, God's power does not exist to solve *our* problems, but to do *his* will. Verse 11 gives the sense of

God doing things now, in the present. God is seen to be the One who who guides all things according to his own will (*Concordance de la Bible*); as the *New International Version* puts it, 'the plan of him who works out everything in accordance with the purpose of his will.'

These better translations help to point us towards the way in which God is at work today. He is 'working things out' at the moment, and at every moment. He is creative, and he is constantly creating.

Question 3 (10 minutes)

In fours

Try to share one example from each of your own lives, where in the midst of problems or pressures you have found or experienced God creating something new. Did this lead you on to a stronger awareness of God, or of what he is like?

Together

Briefly discuss what these examples suggest to you about God.

Suffering and reconciliation

To become more aware of God's suffering, and to explore the power of active suffering to reconcile and reform the world's damage.

Suffering and discipleship

In Session 2 we asked whether God's power is aimed at protection or at creation, and saw that Jesus directs us to his power through creating, particularly when creating a new order or rule – the Kingdom of God. Jesus spoke again and again of the ways in which the Kingdom is breaking into the old familiar world. Many of Jesus's miracles, such as the feeding of the 5000 and 4000, were important not only as signs of mere power but also as signs of a new order for a new Israel (see, for example, Mark 8:14–21).

In the synoptic Gospels (Mark, Matthew and Luke) these miracles are placed alongside the records of conversations with the disciples, in which Jesus warned them that he had to suffer. It emerges very clearly from these Gospels that Jesus saw his own path into this new Kingdom as one of suffering (Mark 8:31f., 9:31f., 10:33f.).

Sharing in Christ's suffering

It might be tempting to say that it was Jesus – and *only* Jesus – who had to suffer as a final sacrifice to propitiate an angry God, so that his followers would then be free for blessings and happiness. Some groups of Christians today would agree with this view, and thus preach a gospel of prosperity to anyone who commits themselves to Jesus Christ. Yet it is precisely at the points in the Gospels where

Jesus speaks of his own suffering, that he *also* begins to call his disciples to a similar lifestyle: 'Anyone who would come after me must deny himself, take up his cross and follow me' (Mark 8:34); and to James and John, 'Yes, you will drink the cup [of suffering] I drink …'(Mark 10:39).

Paul and other letter writers in the early Church were bold enough to say, 'I rejoice in my sufferings for you, and fill up in my flesh what is still lacking in regard to Christ's afflictions' (for example, Colossians 1:24, Romans 5:3); 'we are heirs of God and co-heirs with Christ, if indeed we share in his sufferings in order that we may share in his glory' (for example, Romans 8:17, Philippians 1:29).

Here we can begin to see that in Christ, and thereafter in Christianity, 'suffering' has taken on a very new meaning. The way of Jesus is not to complain about suffering, or to seek to avoid it. The way of Jesus is to look for the coming of a new order of life, breaking into this present one, and to be ready to lead the old world with its suffering into this new regime. Jesus brought about that suffering which in Sessions 1 and 2 we briefly referred to as an 'active' suffering, a way of facing people and events which, far from offering protection from pain and death, transforms them – a transformation which we now consider.

Not suffering for its own sake

Many thousands of Christians in the early years of the Church's history were persecuted by the Roman Empire and the Jews. Similar persecutions and martyrdoms are happening today in places like southern Sudan. In the New Testament, the words for 'suffering' often refer to the persecution, humiliation and rejection experienced by Christians. Jesus saw clearly that if we live at the level of God's new order of life and love in this present world, we are bound to provoke a hostile reaction. Suffering, therefore, is a part of the 'way' that a disciple of the Kingdom chooses. It is not sought, but it must be expected as a consequence of proclaiming the Good News of Jesus, and living in his new community of the Church.

This does not mean that there are two kinds of suffering: the familiar accidents, earthquakes, and man-made wars and cruelties; and a kind of 'heroic persecution'. Suffering is the disease of creation, including humanity's own destructiveness. There is always a breakdown in the goodness of the world when, for example, Christians are persecuted for their faith; or when Satan inflicted ill on Job; or when God cursed Adam, Eve and the serpent. What *is* new is that there is joy even in these sufferings. The whole of life has changed.

Question 1 (12 – 15 minutes)

On your own

'Anyone who would come after me must deny himself, take up his cross and follow me' (Mark 8:34). What does this mean to you? Make a few notes and decide, if you can, to ask God to further open this way of Jesus for you when you pray.

In fours

Discuss some of the ways in which churches, both congregations and national bodies, try to avoid suffering. What would you like to do about this in your own church?

The reconciling work of God

The Old Testament prophets frequently conveyed the heartache which God felt over Israel's love affairs with false gods. It was given to Isaiah (the second prophet, in fact, to use that name) to convey God's will to suffer in the person of a *Suffering Servant*; the person who in four great passages is sometimes spoken of as the people of Israel, and sometimes as a single figure who would redeem Israel by bearing its sins, bringing God's justice and salvation to the Gentiles and the whole earth (Isaiah 42:1–4; 49:1–6; 50:4–9; 52:13–53:12).

Of course, the hope conveyed in Isaiah conveys how fully God feels for his people; it does not convey that God himself would come and experience suffering as human beings do. That further step is only revealed in Jesus.

We have already seen that suffering is not being 'glorified' for its own sake. It is not a bracing treatment for self-improvement! God suffers, because it is in this way that God changes things. It has an aim, it is positive and active. In the light of this, we now ask: How does such suffering change things? What does it achieve? Is it really necessary?

Active suffering places relationships at the top; nothing matters more than overcoming divisions, proud separations, individual needs or preferences and replacing them with a unity of purpose under God's rule. This is why Jesus, uniquely among religious leaders, gave such importance to 'loving one's enemy'. Even if you don't like someone, even if they are attacking you, seek to bring them into a new relationship with you and with God. The 'enemy' may not be human. The 'last enemy' is death itself, and there are many forces and impersonal powers which Christ is still reconciling to God.

Jesus did not just win over death, he won it *over*. The popular religious expression 'the victory of the Cross' can be misleading. What God has achieved in the death of Jesus is a victory of reconciliation, not of conquest.

The work of love is more than victory; the work of atonement more than eradicating the enemy. Jesus, having taught his disciples to love their enemies, continued to love the enemy; he entered the place of death, so cut off from God, and gave voice to its cry, 'My God, my God, why have you forsaken me?'; and in speaking its words he brought it into relationship with God.

Question 2 (15 minutes)

On your own

All of us know people and organisations whom we view with suspicion or dislike, or who 'mean trouble' for us. It may be a matter of beliefs, physical or psychological illness, or personal priorities. For various reasons, such people and organisations – and their illnesses – have a kind of negative hold on us; they are 'principalities and powers' in our lives. We spend a lot of time and energy trying to prove ourselves right or successful against them.

Identify one or two examples for yourself. Rather than merely trying to get on with them in a superficial way, look for some signs of God's life and goodness in them. Imagine speaking about these signs to them. Spend a quiet moment praying for them.

In threes

Discuss some of the ways in which people can come together and be helped to view each other as children of God. Ask how you can give more time to meeting people in these ways.

Living out the reconciliation today

Jesus's lifestyle and death were exactly what life in the glory of God in the Kingdom will be like. God wants us to be like himself – totally self-giving. So what he gives us is what has been accomplished in the life and death of his Son – a reconciliation of all things, a unity or atonement ('at-one-ment').

In many New Testament passages (for example, 2 Corinthians 5:15–18, Ephesians 2:13–16), we see how the Church began to view the Cross (Jesus's death) as not merely an event in the past, but as the reality of Christian life today. This is why, as we noted in Session 1, the New Testament speaks of God's final victory as lying in the future, not in the past.

However, active suffering is more than just a temporary stage in Christian life, prior to the new life of the Kingdom to come. Active suffering is reconciliation. It is at the heart of what the Kingdom life *is* (and will be): 'I fill up in my flesh what is still lacking in regard to Christ's afflictions, for the sake of his body, which is the church' (Colossians 1:24).

Resurrection is happening now, as people are sufficiently united with Christ to continue his reconciling work. Indeed, belief in the Resurrection is expressed and lived out in a readiness to 'win' by reconciling work, rather than by conquering or proving others wrong and oneself right. Reconciliation, even at the political or social level, is a good indicator of God's presence and work.

Question 3 (10 minutes)

In fours

Discuss Romans 8:17 in the light of this Session. What practical changes in your life – changes in attitude or in behaviour, or both – might you begin to make in response to this? Note them down.

Together

Share some of your hopes and insights.

Self-giving and prayer

AIM

To recognise the central place of self-giving in active suffering, and to explore what it means to pray to God to intervene or to heal.

Going into the heart of suffering

Simone Weil, in her extraordinary life of identifying with suffering people before and during the Second World War, knew both illness and cruel manual work. She constantly sought to enter the heart of great suffering; and she wrote:

God is not satisfied with finding his creation good. He wants it also to find itself good. So long as the play of circumstances around us leaves us more or less intact, we more or less believe that the world is created or controlled by ourselves. Affliction [total suffering] reveals, suddenly and to our very great surprise, that we are totally mistaken. After that, if we praise, it really is God's creation that we are praising.
(*GATEWAY TO GOD*, P. 97, FONTANA BOOKS, 1974)

Weil is not saying that suffering has the *purpose* of humbling us. Viewed in this way, therefore, we would have to say suffering is a poor tutor; many people find that suffering only leads to bitterness, withdrawal and pride. Instead, Weil is pointing us to the centre of the attitude of faith, in which one seeks the Cross – the sign of God's presence and activity – even in extreme suffering.

In faith, we become increasingly eager to seek God's presence and activity around us. God found his creation good (for example, Genesis 1:31); yet the creation did not simply rest in his love and enjoy Sabbath with him, but rebelled. Creation, under the stewardship of its created people, has still to 'own' its godliness and goodness, and there is a powerful truth in the portrayal in Genesis of a world that suffers and hurts itself *because it has not yet seen itself as God sees it.*

In Session 3, suffering was called the disease of creation, a self-inflicted disease. In this century, secularism has become a widespread enlargement of the proud independence from God which Adam and Eve displayed. Gabriel Marcel rightly summarised this attitude of modern secularism in the sentence, 'I want to run my own life'. However, the disease is more than a desire for independence. Suffering is the inability of creation (that is, people and the created world we are supposed to care for) to see itself as God sees it.

Reconciliation: discovering God's view

Active suffering means treating the creation as 'good', by entering its agonies and looking for God's view of it all, and then by helping the creation to see things in the same way, reconciling it to his will and way. The process of growing in understanding is not something God can force on his creation or his children; like a teacher, a midwife or the father of a prodigal son, he gives some help, then waits for us to discover how to use it before moving on to the next step.

If we are to continue Christ's reconciling work, this means more than 'keeping the peace' in a family or a nation, although these are important signs of God's will. The most vital reconciliation is with God himself, so that people can enter God's way of seeing and living, and be as he sees them to be.

Why does God allow suffering?

The work of atonement is, in one sense, completed by Jesus. He has overcome every barrier, drawing all things toward unity. Yet people must still stretch out their hands and receive the unity he presents in order to become part of it and one with him. Being united with Christ is life-changing, first and foremost because it means *becoming like him*, and then living as he lives. As we are united with Christ he gives us life-changing gifts, but like every gift of God they must be received and used.

Indeed, the whole of creation is waiting for us – God's children – to attain 'freedom and glory' so that we may bring it to freedom itself (Romans 8:21). In a remarkable phrase, Paul speaks of creation being 'subjected to frustration or

nothingness' by God (Romans 8:20). This may or may not be a reference to the narrative of the Fall in Genesis, but it certainly helps us to see that creation is damaging itself – suffering – until it can be brought to see itself as God sees it. God wants his creation to know itself, and live as he sees it to be, out of the freedom of love and not by his might.

God does not want people to suffer. He wants them to grow in love, openness and reconciliation. But in order to grow, they must accept the fact that everyone begins at the bottom – in self-centredness – *or else they will not be ready to decide to leave self behind, and grow.* When someone is suffering, therefore, they will not be helped if other 'friends' around them treat their suffering as an end in itself, which God or even the church ministers are supposed to remove. The work of Christian ministry is to help those who suffer to grow towards God – even if (painfully) they have to be called to let go their 'bleating calf' or 'mewling baby' attitude to their sufferings – and begin to seek the Cross of Christ in them.

Question 1 (10 minutes)

In threes

Recall examples from your life or from novels, films, etc., where someone has clung on to their suffering either by refusing any help or by using it as an accusation or excuse against other people. How would you help them now?

Share any examples, if you can, where you yourself have been led out of a self-centred 'mewling baby' attitude to your situation. How were you helped?

Together

Share any general points which have developed.

Going down to God

The question 'Why does God allow suffering?' is, of course, where almost everyone begins their exploration of the subject. As we go further into it, however, we are finding a different, more Christ-like understanding – less of 'suffering' and more of '*God*'. As Moltmann observed, Christians must become more concerned not only with 'deifying Christ' (proclaiming his divinity in the face of humanist criticism), but even more with 'Christianising God'. In other words, knowing Jesus actually changes the meaning of the word 'God'. For Christians, God cannot be viewed as remote, aloof, or indeed 'almighty' in the strict sense of the term. Through Jesus, we see that God is even now entering the places of suffering, continuing his work of reconciliation.

This brings us to a surprise. If we wish to seek God's presence, we will find him where he is most active: namely, on the margins, among the poor and suffering (for example, Matthew 25:35–36,40).

In this century, there has been a consistent change of direction in the world-wide Church, recognising through Jesus that God has a 'bias to the poor'. Jesus, having God's nature, became a slave (Philippians 2:6–7), in order to live out the work of reconciliation. We, too, are called to go towards him there, not because the poor or suffering are better people, but because the only way to grow in the life of God is to grow downwards, towards the least loved in creation.

Suffering is not a problem for God. He has, in Christ, turned it into the place of his solution.

Suffering and self-giving

Active suffering involves self-giving to an extraordinary degree. To suffer others willingly and actively (not just people, but everything in creation) means making yourself available to them, meeting with them, and laying yourself open to them, concealing or protecting nothing of yourself. At the same time, this does not mean letting them walk all over you like a doormat! The purpose of such openness is to give them access to the gifts of God, to the work of God in your own life.

For some martyrs of the early Church, persecution led to an astonishing freedom to give glory to God. Even in this century, soldiers about to shoot Christian prisoners have been brought to conversion by their words of forgiveness. Self-giving does not, let us emphasise, mean simply 'pouring everything out on to the table', namely, hopes and fears or joys and hurts. It means giving your own awareness of God, giving yourself inasmuch as you are yourself reconciled to God.

What Jesus gives to us is his own ability (God's ability) to give ourselves completely without losing ourselves and burning out. God does not want his children to burn out, to give up all we are and have nothing left. Entering the world's sufferings constantly would simply be an exercise in heroism if people did it for themselves. One can keep going for a while; then there has to be a respite. So the important step for us to take is to give more time to receiving from God. The more we receive this ability from God, the more we become able to give ourselves as liberally as he does.

Receiving in order to give away

Such receiving is often, rightly, called renewal. However, personal renewal so often stops at the level of receiving gifts from the Spirit, gifts to an individual which he or she is then called to use *for the building up of the body of Christ* (for example, 1 Corinthians 14:12, Ephesians 4:12), including adding new life and people to the body. When it stops in oneself, it is all too easy for one to become possessive and proud about one's gifts. Movements of spiritual renewal are welcome and wonderful gifts to the Church, but unfortunately they can sometimes be greeted by Christians with a self-serving desire for continuous 'spiritual experiences'.

Personal renewal must lead to a new generosity with oneself, or it is a gift which does not bear fruit – something Jesus roundly denounced. When Christians put their own needs first, and demand to have them met, they are behaving like babies indulging a fantasy of their own omnipotence. In their freedom of will, people can only be reconciled to God, and to other people, when they value God's activity and life – that is, his Kingdom – more than their own needs. The aim of the ministry of reconciliation is to bring them towards this change in value.

Question 2 (10 minutes)

In twos

Discuss how you have received signs of reconciliation with God.

- Have you responded by becoming more committed to building up the body of Christ?
- Have you also kept them for yourself?
- What would release you for even greater generosity?

Quietly pray in twos or as a group for this release to come.

How, then, do we pray?

What, therefore, is the place of prayer in this ministry of reconciliation? Does God intervene in his world supernaturally? Since Jesus certainly healed people, should we not pray harder for sufferings to be healed?

A moment's thought shows us that the way *we* pray to God shows what we believe and expect *him* to be like. If we have come to see what he is like in a new way, then that must change the way we pray to him, what we may properly expect him to do, and what we recognise him as doing in the world.

Our praying is all too often the area of our Christian life where we remain the most 'me-centred'. (Remember the example in Session 1 of a man rejoicing that God had spared him from a plane crash, while not even bothering to ask why God had been less generous with the many who *had* been killed.)

This raises a central question about prayer and what we thereby expect of God: what *kind* of God are we seeking to trust? Is he a God who will rearrange many people's lives to suit one person, yet who apparently allowed the Jewish prisoners of the Holocaust to be butchered in their millions?

What may we ask for?

When he has shown his disciples how they should pray (in the Lord's Prayer), Jesus adds: 'Which of you fathers, if your son asks for a fish, will give him a snake instead? Or if he asks for an egg, will you give him a scorpion? If you then, though you are wicked, know how to give good gifts to your children, how much more will your Father in heaven give the Holy Spirit to those who ask him?' (Luke 11:11–13).

As we know from everyday experience, God does not always give people what they ask for. However, when God answers prayer, the answer is always the *Holy Spirit*. What he gives is invariably his own Spirit, God's way of living, operating in many distinct ways and more effectively in some part of our lives or the lives of those we have prayed for. Usually, when someone has been prayed for a great deal, and subsequently becomes aware of 'the power of prayer', what they mean is the love and life of God surrounding them – the presence of God's Spirit – rather than any achievements in persuasion. To receive the answer of the Holy Spirit does not mean that one can ask for anything, and God will give it. When we ask God to intervene in a case of suffering, illness or misfortune, he will listen *for the voice of his Spirit praying through us.*

God's responses to our prayers may indeed include some changes in the circumstances of the world around us; they may include physical healing, for example, or they may not. The test of answered prayer is not our exultation in getting what we want, but that a greater self-giving and generosity can now be seen to occur. It need not be doubted that when we pray, healings sometimes happen. Indeed, other miraculous changes may also occur. As we respond to a case of another's suffering, it is certainly right to pray to God for healing. But, as healers like Francis McNutt and John Wimber emphasise, what matters most to

God is wholeness of relationship with him, the unity of reconciliation. Intercessors learn to ask what it is that God is already doing in someone, and will then bless God for it and seek to co-operate with him.

When we pray, therefore, it is not problem solving in the world for which Jesus wants us to seek help. In whatever situation we are concerned about, our prayer should be simple: 'Father, your Kingdom come on this person or situation. Show us the signs of your reconciling work.'

Question 3 (10 minutes)

In threes

Discuss the ways in which you usually pray, both on your own and with others, and also when your church worships. What differences would it make to pray 'Your Kingdom come' in the situations you are praying for?

Together

Share any insights or observations.

CONCLUSIONS

A faith based on the belief that God's way is fully revealed in Jesus is not a theory which you can believe in while tentatively waiting to see how things turn out. God's power to reconcile all things into new and eternal life is not something to be watched from the sidelines. You can't get the feel of it, or begin to see how powerful it is, by hedging your bets and wondering if it will work. The question with which this course has been concerned – Why does God allow suffering? – is one raised from the sidelines of life with God. We have found ourselves led gradually towards a life lived with Christ's own passion and can begin to answer the question only by getting closer to Jesus, and to the God which Jesus fully reveals to us.

At the heart of the answer which has emerged is a fresh awareness of creation's longing and limits, which Paul so wonderfully expresses in Romans 8. God sees the world – including its people – as good, in much the way in which a mother regards her new baby – or, indeed, her unborn baby – as good, even if other people already see the difficulties! The 'good creation' is nonetheless a vast collection of self-centred and isolated parts; as God's world damages itself, like squabbling infants and pets unwilling to grow up or to be guided or used by the hands of more mature children of God, suffering is the result.

God, with heart-breaking patience, continually gives it new opportunities to learn and grow; he suffers its follies and pains in order to reconcile it with himself, and let it see and know itself to be his good creation, so that it may start to live as such. When God's children are filled with the mind of Christ, as the Kingdom comes, they will be more alert and caring guides, prepared to enter the places of suffering and to shepherd the world into a more mature unity.

God is at work in his world, fashioning new life in the midst of the old. His kingdom is breaking in. There are centres of reconciliation, 'islands of God's generosity' in the middle of chaotic seas. He wants us to step with greater commitment into communities of self-giving and receiving; giving ourselves fully and being led to share in Christ's sufferings and in his glory.

Conclusion

On your own

List some of the main points you have understood or appreciated from the course. Note any practical actions you want to take as a result of working through the course with your colleagues.

Together

Conclude by giving thanks together for any new awareness of God which has come to you during the course.